MINECRAFT

A Beginner's Guide

David Oconner

©Copyright 2012 David Oconner

ISBN-13: 978-1475239744

D0191710

Table of Contents

Minecraft

History

Minecraft is block-infested sandbox building/exploring game developed by Mark Persson, aka 'Notch', and his company, Mojang AB. The 'full version' or Minecraft has been available on PC since November 18th, 2011, but the game has been popular since Beta testing opened to players in 2009.

Controls

Esc - Pause/Menu
Left Mouse Button – Primary Action (Dig/Chop/Attack) ; Single-tap – Toggle Doors/Switches
Right Mouse Button – Secondary Action (Use/Place Block/Interact/Eat)
WASD – Move/Strafe (Double-tap 'W' to Sprint)
Space – Jump (Can be held)
Mouse – Look
Left Shift   Sneak (Also keeps you from accidentally falling)
'I' – Inventory
Mouse Button 3 ('Mouse Scroll Button') – Cycle through inventory (1-9)
'Q' – Drop Item
Tab – (Multiplayer) – Players List

HUD

Heads Up Display

1) Health – Shown by hearts – Hearts are removed when damage is taken from: falling, monster attacks, fire/lava, poison, explosions and drowning/suffocating.

2) Armor – Shown as little grey tunics above your health – Armor icons only show up when you're wearing protective, craftable armor, made of leather, iron, gold, or diamond. Each armor icon indicates how much damage will be absorbed from attacks (damage from drowning, fire, suffocation are not reduced). Each tunic indicates about an 8% decrease in damage taken.

3) Hunger – Shown by 'drumsticks' – Indicates how 'full' you are – When you are full (or nearly full) you will regenerate health as normal and can sprint – When your hunger gets low, you will no longer regenerate health (hearts) or be able to sprint. You become hungry at a slow rate as you play, but some actions make you hungrier faster, like: attacking, sprinting and jumping.

4) Experience – The Green bar with sections – the number in the middle indicates what 'Level' you are. You gain experiences by killing monsters/animals, shown as little green orbs that drop when they die. You can use experience to enchant your tools and

items. (See the enchanting section for more details.)

5) Inventory Quick-slots: The 9 empty boxes in your inventory can be filled with any item in your inventory and is useful for quickly switching between regularly used items, like cobblestone, pickaxes or food. You can access each slot by pressing its corresponding number key (1-9) or by using the mouse wheel (mouse button 3) to cycle through the quick-slots.

6) Air -Only shown while underwater/suffocating- Bubbles will appear above your 'Hunger' icons. These show you how much air you have left. When you run out of air, you'll start taking drowning damage at the rate of roughly 1 heart-per-second. Get your head above water to get more air. You can also suffocate by being crushed by sand, your hearts reducing quickly.

Minecraft Basics

So what the heck can I do in this weird, block-ridden game?

Placing and Picking up Blocks

Most blocks in Minecraft can be picked up, but not always by hand. You'll need special tools to extract precious ores or till the earth to make your first farm. In general, though left-click will dislodge blocks and right-click will place them. (You can hold down either for automatic mining/digging/chopping or placement.)

Craft tools and weapons and collect and manufacture your own building materials

Make axes, picks, shovels, swords and more from stone, iron, diamond and even gold!

Explore the snow and ice, mountainous ranges, the seashore, swamp or forests!

Each area has unique plants and animals!

Above ground you'll find various biomes with plants and animals that only grow/appear in specific regions. Explore snow-covered peaks; blistering, cactus-filled deserts; dense jungles, lush forests and more!

Delve deep underground

Uncover abandoned mineshaft, rare ruined fortresses and deep ravines that expose precious blocks to fearless spelunkers.

There are treasures in the earth, if you know where to look. Strip abanonded mineshafts bare of old rails and be on the look out for aggressive cave spiders!

Explore other dimension.

But be careful, below the bedrock of the surface lies the fiery 'Nether', accessible only through specially-prepared portals. You'll find nether-only blocks and items, fearsome zombie-pigs, massive ghasts, magma cubes and fireball throwing blazes. Explore sprawling nether-fortresses, if you dare: the Nether is not for the faint-hearted.

Can you find 'The End'?

The mysterious Endermen hold the key to the terminal region of Minecraft's gameworld. Explore the Nether for the other piece of the key to activate long-abandoned portals, but beware: there is no turning back.

Your First Day

You're safe during the daylight hours in Minecraftia, but the night is full of danger! Let's get started!

Simple Dirt Marker

Take a moment to get your bearings. The place where you first enter the gameworld is called your 'spawn point'. This is where you'll respawn if you happen to perish (before you sleep in a bed, more on that later) due to an untimely fall or a zombie ambush. Take a look around and try and find some unique landmarks. Until you build some markers of your own, it's very easy to get lost.

Don't stray too far from your spawn, just yet. Until you have some tools and shelter ready, stay within viewing distance of where you first entered the game. When you die in Minecraft, you'll drop all your items and lose your accumulated experience before you respawn. Dropped items decay (disappear from the game forever) about 5 minutes after they leave your inventory, so it's important that you not stray too far. It's nerve-wracking to have only only precious seconds to locate and recover your tools and block before they are gone forever because you died too far from your spawn.

Keep an eye on the sky. Minecraftia's sun travels from east to west, just like our own, but it does so much faster than ours: a day is only 10 minutes long! When the sun is directly overhead, you'll know you only have about 5 minutes until sundown. Work quickly!

Okay! I know where I am and that time is short! What now?

Trees

One word: Wood. Your #1 priority should be to procure a good source of lumber from (hopefully) nearby trees . If you've spawned in a forest or mountainous area you should find some nearby (remember to turn up your view distance if you're having trouble). If not, you may have to scout the area to find some lumber.

Okay, you found a tree: now punch it! (Hint: click and hold your Left Mouse buttons for optimal tree-punching). After a few hits, you should have a block of wood! Congrats! Gather up a couple trees' worth of blocks (10 or so blocks) and we'll move on:

Inventory Use And Crafting

Press 'I' and open up for inventory. It should look something like this:

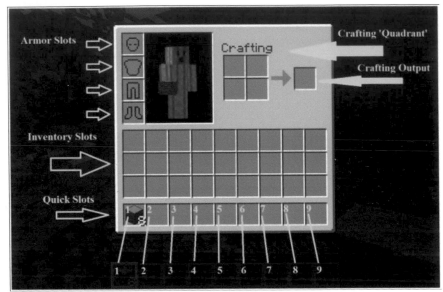

Heads Up Display

Once your inventory is open you'll see a couple different sections: in the mid-left, you'll see your character. To the left of that you'll see the 4 armor slots, arranged vertically. This is where you can put on craftable armor-pieces that can shield you from damage. Below your character will be 30 inventory slots. This is where you'll carry all your blocks, items, armor, food and everything else you can carry. Below the inventory slots are your quick-use slots. You'll want to put items you use frequently here so you can access them without having open up your inventory. (Put the items you use more in the 1, 2, 3, 4 slots, as they are going to be the easiest to reach, just above your left-hand on the WASD controls.)

To the right of your character is the crafting-quadrant. (Really, just 4 slots, but 'quadrant' sounds cooler) You can craft small items within your inventory by placing different items in the proper configurations in craft-quadrant and, if you've got the crafting recipe right, the new item to be crafted will appear on the single box to the right of the arrow.

The recipe we are interested in now is the '*Workbench*'. To make a workbench, you'll need 4 wooden planks. How do you get wooden planks? Put that wood we cut down earlier in the crafting-quadrant – it becomes 4 planks of wood!

Planks Of Wood

Well done! Now, put one plank of wood in each of the four quadrants – you can now make a workbench! Click on the bench to create it, then place it in your inventory.

Crafting Table

The workbench is where you'll make most of your tools, weapons, armor and more. There are dozens of recipes, and some even work with different components, for now, let's just focus on the one we need: a pickaxe.

To make a *pickaxe*, we'll need 3 planks of wood and two sticks. You already know how to make that, so go ahead and turn the rest of your gathered wood into planks. Now, we need sticks:

stack 2 plank of wood vertically on top of one another, so they're occupying 2 slots – viola! Sticks! Make sure you make a least 3.

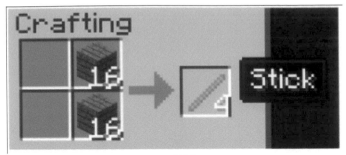

Sticks

Let's go ahead and place that Workbench. Don't worry too much about where, you can pick it up when you're done, if you want.

After it's placed, right click on it. You should see a a crafting-quadrant, except with 6 slots, (a crafting sextant?). This is where you'll make most of your tools, weapons, building materials, etc. For now, let's get that pickaxe made. Take your sticks and your wood planks and arrange them like so: Click on the pick! You can now mine!

Wood Pickaxe

Let's get to digging! Start digging one block down, then forward, then down then forward. Digging like this makes a nice natural staircase to the surface, and it keeps you from falling to your door should you open up a natural cavern beneath your blocky feet. Keep digging until you reach Stone. It looks like this:

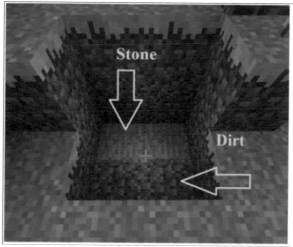

Stone vs Dirt

Mine about 2 dozen or so blocks and then head back to your craft bench (or drop it, if you've picked it up). It's time to upgrade your tools! Go ahead and make another pickaxe, but, this time, replace the Wood Planks with Cobblestone. There you go! You've made a Stone Pickaxe!

Stone Pickaxe

Stone tools dig/cut/chop/scoop faster than Wooden tools and also last longer! (Then next tool upgrade is Iron, but let's not worry about that, for now.)

Let's make a Stone Shovel, a Stone Axe (for cutting wood) and a Stone Sword, for fighting off monsters in the dark.

Stone Shovel

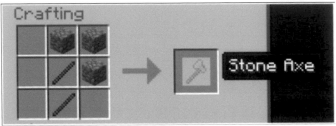

Stone Axe

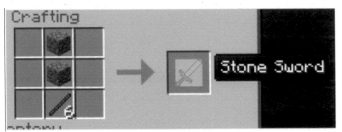

Stone Sword

Now that we've got some tools, let's start taming the darkness.

Let There Be Light

There are several types of light sources in Minecraft, but the one we're most concerned about now (and the one you're sure to use most of the time) is: Torches. Torches are made of sticks and coal, like so:

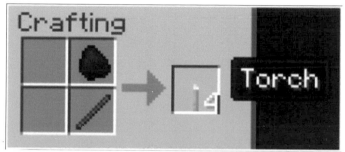

Torch

(The recipe for torches is small enough that you can make them easily without a workbench.)

You already know how to get sticks, so let's find coal. This is what you're looking for:

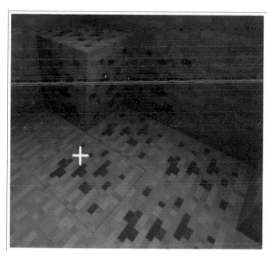

Coal

Coal is found anywhere you find Stone. If you're spawned in a hilly or mountainous area, you might luck out and be able to see coal seams on the surface. If not, scout around your immediate area and look for some easily accessible Coal blocks. If not, it's time to dig. Use the same Dig Down/Dig Forward/Dig Down routine as before. This will keep you safe from deadly falls and able to climb back up easily.

If you've got a reasonable supply of coal (20-30 pieces), you're ready to start building your first shelter! (If no coal is visible anywhere, head back and start chopping down some more trees. It's a little time-consuming, but we can make charcoal, instead. We'll see how in a minute.)

Your First Shelter

Now that you've got your tools and some torches, let's get you a base camp set up. What we want to accomplish with this first house is to keep you safe during the night, set up a compact workstation, complete with a Workbench, at least one Furnace/Smelter, and a couple storage Chests, and then we can start on your first mineshaft!

A great site for your first shelter will be:
- At least a few blocks away from water (Avoid those pesky floods!),
- A few blocks away from any obvious cliffs or caverns,
- Preferably away from sand (Digging can be slow and falling sand can suffocate you!),
- Visible from spawn and from multiple angles,
- Near at least one or two trees,
- Within walking distance of a water source.

Build your shelter out of either cobblestone or wood planks. Why? Neither of these blocks are found underfoot, are easily to see from a distance and are good at resisting explosive damage (oh, and there will be explosions!) if you get lost or are returning from a long expedition.

Build the outside walls as a 5x5 square perimeter, with one column open where you want your door to go. After you've finished the first level, hop on top of the wall and build another two blocks high, it should look like this (I used cobblestone):

Wall

Hop down into the structure and fill in the top level above you. Once you've added this ceiling, drop your Workbench and we'll craft a Furnace, like so:

Furnace

Furnaces are used to cook food, smelt ore into useful metal, make glass and more. After the Workbench, Furnaces are probably the most import block in Minecraft. If you're lacking coal (or just curious), make some charcoal now with Wood Planks and Wood, here:

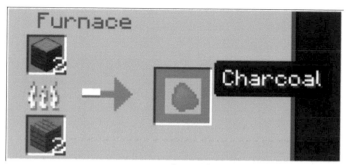

Charcoal

Let there be light! Go ahead and open up your inventory or Workbench and make some torches, if you haven't already. Put one or two inside your new house and one on each of the outer sides.

By now, the sun is probably setting and your doorway is bare! Let's get you a door! Craft one with 6 planks of Wood in this configuration:

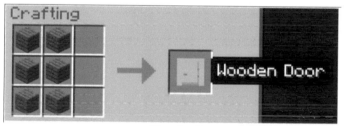

Wooden Door

Select the Door and right-click on the empty ground in your doorway. There we go! It's a bit cramped, but it's home.

Safe from the Darkness... Now what? Now that you're safe, let's talk about what goes bump in the dark.

Monsters

I told you nighttime was scary, right? Here's why: *monsters.* You may be able to explore and build without a care during the daytime (unless you fall off something high or set yourself on fire or... just be careful, okay?), but at night the is filled with things that want you dead.

Why the night? Monsters in Minecraft spawn (pop into the word) in low-light conditions. When you finally start mining, you'll find caves and even your mineshafts crawling with baddies, if you're not careful. Staying it well-lit areas, like your house (you did remember to put torches out, right?) will keep you safe, but you can't cower in your house forever. Let's see what you're up against:

Creepers: The deadliest thing on 4-legs; these green, eye-less monsters are silent until they're within arm's reach... and by then it's too late! Creepers are the suicide bombers of Minecraftia. They don't 'attack', per se, but sneak up on unwary miners and explore, destroying nearby blocks and objects. The only sounds creepers make is when they fall far enough to far damage, or when they emit their tell-tale 'hiiisssss', just before they explode.

Either kill them from a distance with your bow or use hit-and-run knockback attacks (double tap 'forward' and attack while running) to wear down their health without staying close enough for them to explode! (Creepers can linger even after the sun comes up. Keep an eye out!)

Skeletons: The dead walk... and shoot a bow? Skeletons come from out of the darkness with an urge to practice their undead archery on you, if you come too close! These skeletal archers can be dangerous for a couple reasons: all they need is line-of-site to pelt you with arrows that cause damage and knockback from over a dozen blocks away. Single skeletons are a nuisance, but if you're caught out in the open, you can soon have arrows coming from all directions! Either rush into melee range and start hacking at them with your sword, or tactically return fire with your own bow to stop them. (Skeletons cannot survive in direct sunlight, but will retreat under trees and in water during the day.)

Zombies: Like zombies everywhere else, these guys just want to walk straight for you and eat your brains. Zombies will take the most straight-forward path towards you and won't stop until you're dead! A few arrows or sword-hits will drop them, but they usually aren't alone. Dispatch them quickly to avoid becoming surrounded. (Like Skeletons, Zombies will die in direct sunlight. Thankfully, they aren't nearly as good at finding shade.)

Spiders: These 8-legged menaces can't fit through small doorways, but they don't need to: they can just climb over the walls! Spiders can sense you behind walls and will climb up and over to pounce on you! Pelting these hissing arachnids with arrows from your bow is your best-bet. They are a wider than other monsters and not terribly fast and easy to hit. Spiders become non-aggressive in daylight.

Endermen: The rare Enderman (singular) is passive, but creepily tall creature. They will generally ignore you and busy themselves by moving single blocks around seemingly at random, as long as you don't look them in the eyes. Once you make eye-contact, be ready to fight! Endermen pack a serious punch and can teleport short distances and have no problem appearing behind you to attack. Make sure you're armored before you try to ambush one: they can't be killed by arrows (they just teleport out of the way) and hit hard, so make sure you're ready for an intense battle. Endermen are damaged by water and will quickly teleport to safety when it rains.

Underground

You'll be stalked by skeletons, creepers and zombies underground, but there are a few monsters that only dwell deep beneath the earth.

Slimes

Slimes

Slimes are very rare, and fairly harmless, but they're persistent. Slimes only spawn very deep underground and come in a variety of sizes. Most slimes are smaller than you, but massive versions exist that can be the size of your first shelter! Slimes can't actually hurt you, but when they get close enough, they'll push you around until you kill them all. Don't engage them near lava, cliffs or creepers. (Slimes drop 'slimeballs', which can be made cool 'sticky pistons'. Make sure and collect them whenever you can!)

Cave Spiders

Cave Spiders

It's another spider! This one is smaller, meaner and much more aggressive than its above-ground cousin. Cave spiders only spawn in abandoned mineshafts, but even a pair of them can be very dangerous. You'll know a cave spider-nest is about when you find gobs of cobwebs covering the walls and ceilings. (Make sure you always have a sword handy to cut your way out of the webs!) Cave spiders are fast enough that using a bow isn't always recommended. When fighting one, keep an eye out for other monsters, as these mean arachnids are rarely found alone.

Now you know what lurks in the dark (but not in the Nether)... who cares! Let's mine!

Mining!

It's not just stone that you'll find underground, though you'll find plenty of that, but useful iron and gold ore, precious diamonds and even redstone (used for making circuitry and mechanical devices), and nigh-unbreakable obsidian, from which you can make a gateway to The Nether!

I'm not going to give away everything, but I've included some must-know facts below and some neat recipes to help you get started mining underground.

There's lots to see under, but lots of ways to get trapped, killed, lost or incinerated. Here are some basic tips:

- **Never dig straight down**!

Unless you know precisely what is under you (and most of the time you don't), avoid digging straight down unless you don't mind falling to your death. Sure, you'll be fine 95% of the time, but one long drop in lava and all your items are gone!

- **Never dig straight-up!**

This isn't nearly as dangerous as digging straight down, but digging straight up is a good way to drop sand blocks on your head (sand doesn't hold itself up), flood your mine or accidentally dig straight into some lava. If you see drips of red (lava) or (blue) coming from the blocks overhead, think twice before digging into them.

- **Always bring food!**

Starving to death is never fun. Starving to death lost and confused in your own mine is embarrassing and a great way to lose all the stuff in your inventory. Bring at least a couple food items down into the mine to snack on so you can regenerate your health if you get attacked.

- **Always bring light!**

Can you mine in the dark? Sure, if you want to be swarmed by monsters. Remember: monsters spawn in the darkness and it's easy to get lost.

- **Don't be stingy with the lights!**

If you make sure and dot your underground walls with a torch every 6 or 7 blocks, you should be able to make your supplies of torches last a while and keep your mine (largely) free of pesky creepers and zombies.

- **Always bring a weapon!**

You can fight without a sword or a bow, but you'll get hurt and need to eat more often. Don't find yourself fighting for your life far away from home!

- **Always bring wood!**

Almost everything you need can be found underground, with the exception of food and wood. Unless you're exploring an abandoned mineshaft, wood is very scarce underground and you can't make new tools, workbenches or torches without wood. Always carry a stack or so to avoid unnecessary trips to the surface.

- **Always bring a bucket of water!**

Why? Are you going to get thirsty? Nope, but if you step in a lava-pit, you'll be glad you did. Water turns lava into obsidian or cobblestone and can put you out if you catch on fire, Burning to death isn't fun and dying in lava is even worse: all your items (except your diamonds) will be destroyed instantly!

- **Dig Deeper!**

The best ores can only be found near bedrock that separates the Underground from the Nether (How do you get there? Make a gate from Obsidian and light it with a flint and steel. I'll let you figure out the particulars). Diamond and redstone are only found within 20-or-so block from the very bottom of the map!

- **Upgrade your tools!**

Some ores can only be extracted with certain pickaxes. Stone can be broken, but not collected by-hand. Iron ore can only be collected with a stone-or-better pickaxe and gold/diamond can only be collected with an iron-or-better pickaxe. Obsidian is even hard to mine...

- **A compass is a good idea!**

You can build yourself a compass with iron and redstone that will point you back to where you first entered the game. This is handy for point you back to familiar territory when you get turned around exploring underground.

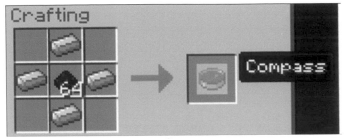

Compass

- **Mark your trails!**

It's easy to get lost underground, but if you mark your trails, you can easily find your way out. I always place torches on the left-hand side of the walls as I explore, so when I get turned around I just have to follow the torches to my right to know I'm headed back in the right (get in?) direction.

Heading In

Heading Out

- **Be (very) careful around lava!**

Glowing red lava can set you on fire with just a touch and, if you take a swim in it, will kill you in seconds! What's worse, if you die in or near lava, the items in your inventory can be destroyed.

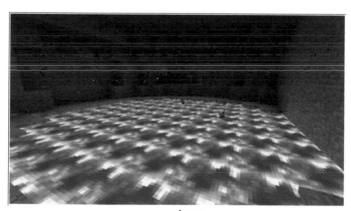

Lava

What to do when you're trapped.

Okay, so you're lost and turned around and you have no idea where 'back' is. You have a couple options: 1) Build a compass: If you have 4 iron ingots and 1 redstone and a crafting table, you can make yourself a compass to show you which way to dig back to spawn. 2) Dig straight up and drop blocks underneath you: This is generally a last-ditch escape effort. It's not recommended except when you're desperate. The only thing worse than losing your items underground is losing them trapped somewhere within a solid block of stone.

Useful Mining Recipes

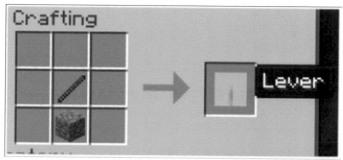

Lever: Try it with a Power Mine Rail!

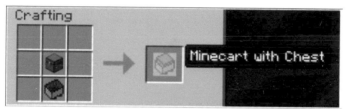

Mobil Storage

A Self-Propelled Minecart! Just add Coal!

Furnace: Turn your ores into ingots!

Minecart: Right Click to Ride the Rails!

Powered Rail: In Minecraftia, rail pushes you! (Try attaching a redstone torch to it!)

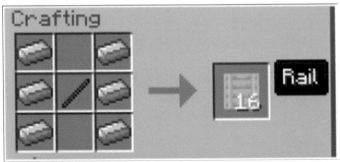

Rails: Just add a mine-cart for fast underground travel!

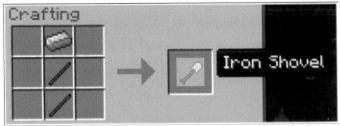

Iron Shovel: Dirt, can you dig it?

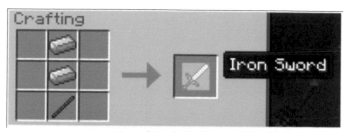

Iron Sword: Back, foul creeper! Back!

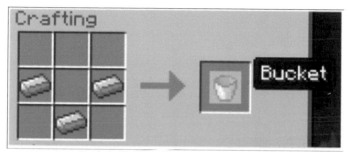

Bucket: Hold and transport water and lava!

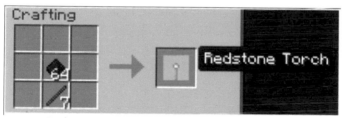

Redstone Torch: Think of it as a magical battery-wand.

Time to Eat!

Oh man! I bet you're hungry! Whenever you run, attack or jump your hunger gauge will drop faster than normal. (You'll eventually get hungry just standing around, but it takes much longer.) There are quite a few ways to keep yourself fed. Let's have a look:

Farming

Growing your own food can be fun! The first thing you'll need it a hoe:

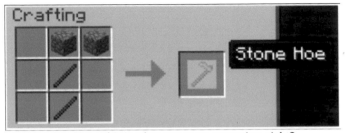

Hoe: This is what you were expecting, right?

Right click on a grassy-dirt block (these are only found in direct sunlight). You'll see the dirt turn into a plowed section of earth. Neat, eh? You'll plant seeds in these patches, but first you'll need some seeds. Head out into your nearest forest or plain and start knocking down tall grasses. You'll eventually get a handful of seeds. Head back to near your shelter and pick a nice sunny patch of ground. (Plants need light to grow. The more light the better.) Hoe the ground and plant your seeds!

All done? Almost. Plants grow fastest when they are near a source of water. Grab a bucket and head to the nearest water source and fill it up. Come back, dig a little trench near your tilled field and dump out the water. You should see your tilled patches turn a darker shade of brown as the water saturates the field!

Now you can wait! In about 5 minutes, under excellent conditions, you should have your first crop of wheat!

Wait, is the wheat ready? Plants grow in stages, from seed to completed crop. If you harvest too early, you won't get any wheat or seeds back. Let's look at the stages of growth:

Wheat Stages

Go ahead and wait until all your wheat is grown and then turn it into some bread!

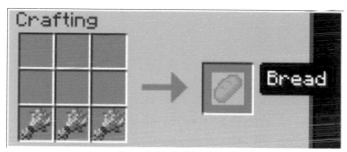

Bread: No baking involved!

Now you're a farmer! Well done!

(You can also grow sugar cane and melons, though these seeds are hard to find...)

Hunting

So you're more of a hunter than a gatherer, eh?

Well, hunting is pretty straight-forward: find a pig, cow, or chicken and kill it. Then cook the meat that drops in a Furnace. Repeat as necessary and eat until you're stuffed.

Cooked meat is much more filling than raw is, but you're welcome to eat either. (Though you might get a stomach-ache from the raw stuff.)

(Oh: you can also breed your own animals for slaughter. Try farming up some wheat and offering to animals. You might also be able to pen them in with fencing, which I'm sure couldn't be made with the right configuration of Sticks...)

Enchanting & Brewing

Enchanting

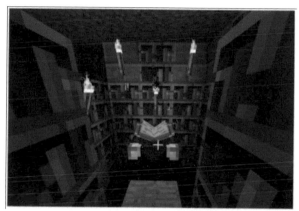

Enchanting Bench: Could those Bookshelves be for more than decoration... ?

Did you know you can make your tools, weapons and armor even better? Remember that experience bar we talked about earlier? (The green segmented-line at the bottom of the screen?) Well, here is where you cash in all that experience for enchantments that make your tools last long and drop more goodies from ore blocks, your weapons sharper and stronger, and your armor protect your from fire and poison.

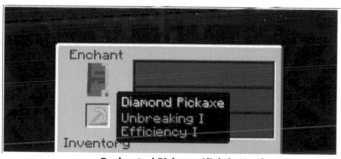

Enchanted Pickaxe: Slightly Used

Once you know how to mine Obsidian, to make bookshelves and have collected some redstone, you'll have everything you need to make an enchanting bench. Again, this guide is more for new players and I don't want to ruin the fun by telling you how to do everything, but you'll find some hints about collecting Obsidian and redstone in the Mining section, and I'll just say now that bookcases are made with wood, and books are made of paper, which is made of sugar. I'll let you figure out the rest. Get to your workbench and start experimenting!

Brewing

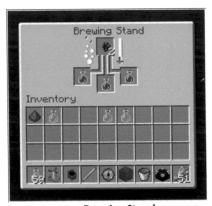

Brewing Stand

Want to make poisons, do you? Well you better get yourself a cauldron (which I'm SURE isn't made out of iron), a brewing stand (which CAN'T be made out of stone and a hard-to find item, called a *cough* blaze rod *cough*, from the Nether), and some bottles (which, incidentally are made from melted glass...).

Well, I don't want to give too much away, but you can find ingredients for you potions all over Minecraftia. From monsters drops, to redstone, to food items and more.

Redstone Circuits

What about Advanced Users?

Redstone Circuit with Repeaters

So you found all that redstone underground and don't know what to do with it. It can't be made into tools, weapons, armor or food, so what the heck is it for?

Try spreading some redstone dust on the ground. See how it spreads out in lines? Redstone dust is the Minecraftia equivalent of wire! Redstone torches (made just like regular torches, except with redstone), along with buttons (made from cobblestone), levels and pressure plates will send a pulse of power to attached resdtone circuits.

But what can you power? Well:

- Doors,
- Powered Rails (see above),
- Pistons,
- Trap doors,
- Dispensers,
- Fence Gates,
- Noteblocks.

Here are some of the more complex recipes to help you get started with your redstone experiments:

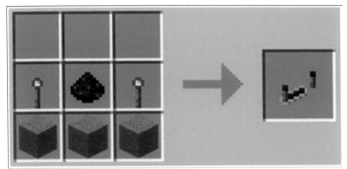

Repeater

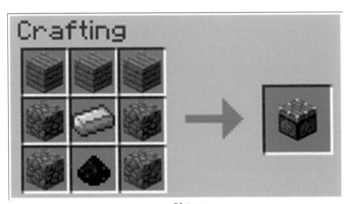

Piston

So... now what?

Minecraft technically has an ending, but most players aren't in any hurry to 'beat' the game.

Updates come along to add new features to the game every couple weeks and playing online is a different type of experience altogether. (In fact, parts of this guide might be outdated already, though most information should be accurate.)

Start up a multiplayer server with some friends, or join one of hundreds of active servers online. There are tons of user-made mods that add new rules and items to turn 'vanilla' Minecraft into a whole new experience. There are zombie-survival servers, RPG servers, Creative servers (where you can build to your heart's content), Hardcore (1-death and that's it) servers, PvP servers and much, much more. Check out the forums on Minecraft.net for more info.

The Mojang team is fairly active on Twitter and occasional stops by the Minecraft sub-Reddit on reddit.com: www.reddit.com/r/minecraft. Get the low-down on new mods, epic buildings and servers that other Minecrafters are working on here.

Want to just build, build, build? Try Creative Mode from the Main Menu. You don't have to worry about dying or monsters and can instantly spawn any type of block, or, animal or monster you want. Build whole cities, ocean liners, skyscrapers, or anything else you can imagine.

Want to try something harder? Hardcore Mode is just like normal Survival (the mode described in this guide), but you only get one life. Just one long fall, one too-many arrows to the head or an unlucky dip in lava and the game is over: upon death your Hardcore world is erased. Sounds serious, right? It's intense. Give it a try if you feel like you've mastered Minecraftia.

###

About The Author

David Oconner has been writing and publishing books on many of his varied interests. He has books on topics such as Cichlid Fish, How to Grow Tomatoes, Sugar Gliders, How to Play Minecraft and more.

CPSIA information can be obtained
at www.ICGtesting.com
Printed in the USA
LVIW011506250912

300297LV00001B